Published by Humble Creek, P.O. Box 719, Uhrichsville, Ohio 44683

Member of the
Evangelical Christian
Publishers Association

Printed in China.

A Mother's Favorite Quotes

Wisdom for Life & Motherhood

HUMBLECREEK
INSPIRATION FOR LIFE

Her children arise up, and call her blessed;
her husband also, and he praiseth her.
Proverbs 31:28

There is in every true woman's heart a spark
of heavenly fire, which lies dormant in the broad
daylight of prosperity, but which kindles up and
beams and blazes in the dark hour of adversity.
Washington Irving

We never know how high we are
Till we are called to rise;
And then, if we are true to plan,
Our statures touch the skies.
Emily Dickinson

From women's eyes this doctrine I derive:
They sparkle still the right Promethean fire;
They are the books, the arts, the academes,
That show, contain, and nourish all the world.
William Shakespeare

There are two ways of spreading light:
to be
The candles or the mirror that reflects it.
Edith Wharton

Who can find a virtuous woman? for her
price is far above rubies.
Proverbs 31:10

A Mother's Favorite Quotes

If the time should ever come when women are not Christians and houses are not homes, then we shall have lost the chief cornerstones on which civilization rests.
Andrew Dickson White

Favour is deceitful, and beauty is vain: but a woman that feareth the LORD, she shall be praised.
Proverbs 31:30

No coward soul is mine,
No trembler in the world's storm-troubled sphere:
I see Heaven's glories shine,
And faith shines equal, arming me from fear.
Emily Brontë

Grow old along with me!
The best is yet to be,
The last of life, for which the first was made.
Our times are in His hand.
Robert Browning

And Jacob served seven years for Rachel;
and they seemed unto him but a few days, for
the love he had to her.
Genesis 29:20

The surest way to get a thing done in this
life is to be prepared for doing without it, to
the exclusion even of hope.
Jane Welsh Carlyle

A Mother's Favorite Quotes

No man is poor who has had a godly mother.
Abraham Lincoln

For whosoever shall do the will of my Father
which is in heaven, the same is my brother, and
sister, and mother.
Matthew 12:50

. . .Intreat me not to leave thee, or to return
from following after thee: for whither thou goest,
I will go; and where thou lodgest, I will lodge:
thy people shall be my people,
and thy God my God.
RUTH
Ruth 1:16

Necessity can set me helpless on my back,
but she cannot keep me there; nor can
four walls limit my vision.
"Michael Fairless"
(Margaret Fairless Barber)

I have been reminded of your sincere faith,
which first lived in your grandmother Lois and
in your mother Eunice and, I am persuaded,
now lives in you also.
2 Timothy 1:5 NIV

A rich child often sits in a
poor mother's lap.
Danish proverb

As unto the bow the cord is,
So unto the man is woman;
Though she bends him, she obeys him,
Though she draws him, yet she follows;
Useless each without the other.
Henry Wadsworth Longfellow

I should not dare to call my soul my own.
Elizabeth Barrett Browning

. . .Martha, Martha, thou art careful and
troubled about many things: But one thing is
needful: and Mary hath chosen that good part,
which shall not be taken away from her.
Luke 10:41–42

All the privilege I claim for my own sex. . .
is that of loving longest, when existence or when
hope is gone.
Jane Austen

Be thou my Vision,
O Lord of my heart;
Nought be all else to me,
Save that Thou art.
Mary Byrne

If you stop to be kind you must swerve often
From your path.
Mary Webb

A Mother's Favorite Quotes

She opens her arms to the poor and extends
her hands to the needy. When it snows, she has
no fear for her household; for all of them are
clothed in scarlet.
Proverbs 31:20–21 NIV

My old father used to have a saying that
"If you made a bad bargain, hug it the tighter."
Abraham Lincoln

Take love when love is given,
But never think to find it
A sure escape from sorrow
Or a complete repose.
Sara Teasdale

I do not own an inch of land,
But all I see is mine.
Lucy Larcom

And there came a certain poor widow, and
she threw in two mites, which make a farthing.
And he. . .saith unto them, . . .For all they
did cast in of their abundance; but she of her
want did cast in all that she had,
even all her living.
Mark 12:42–44

And now, my daughter, fear not; I will do
to thee all that thou requirest: for all the city of
my people doth know
that thou art a virtuous woman.
BOAZ
Ruth 3:11

Women are never stronger than when they
arm themselves with their weaknesses.
Madame du Deffand

A soft answer turneth away wrath.
Proverbs 15:1

All the way my Saviour leads me;
What have I to ask beside?
Can I doubt His tender mercy,
Who through life has been my Guide?
Fanny Crosby

We grow old as soon as we cease
to love and trust.
Madame de Choiseul

She never quite leaves her children at home,
even when she doesn't take them along.
Margaret Culkin Banning

Who ran to help me when I fell,
And would some pretty story tell,
Or kiss the place to make it well?
My mother.
Ann Taylor
(1804)

Marriage, to women as to men, must be a
luxury, not a necessity; an incident of life,
not all of it.
Susan Brownell Anthony

A mother is not a person to lean on, but a
person to make leaning unnecessary.
Dorothy Canfield Fisher

When a woman ceases to alter the fashion
of her hair, you guess that she has passed the
crisis of her experience.
Mary Austin

Every wise woman buildeth her house: but
the foolish plucketh it down with her hands.
Proverbs 14:1

I do not ask for any crown
But that which all may win;
Nor try to conquer any world
Except the one within.
Louisa May Alcott

. . .My soul doth magnify the Lord, and my
spirit hath rejoiced in God my Saviour. For he
hath regarded the low estate of his handmaiden:
for, behold, from henceforth all generations shall
call me blessed.
MARY
Luke 1:46–48

Of all the rights of women, the greatest
is to be a mother.
Lin Yutang

I commend unto you Phebe our sister. . .
that ye receive her in the Lord, as becometh
saints. . .for she hath been a succourer of
many, and of myself also.
Romans 16:1–2

A woman waits for me, she contains all,
nothing is lacking.
Walt Whitman

And all thy children shall be taught
of the LORD; and great shall be
the peace of thy children.
Isaiah 54:13

Women wish to be loved without a why or a
wherefore; not because they are pretty or good,
or well-bred, or graceful, or intelligent,
but because they are themselves.
Henri Frederic Amiel

How many loved your moments of glad grace,
And loved your beauty with love false or true,
But one man loved the pilgrim soul in you,
And loved the sorrows of your changing face.
William Butler Yeats

Hide not your talents, they for use were made,
What's a Sun-Dial in the Shade?
Benjamin Franklin

A Mother's Favorite Quotes

Better by far you should forget and smile
Than that you should remember and be sad.
Christina Georgina Rossetti

Alas! the love of Women! it is known
To be a lovely and a fearful thing.
George Noel Gordon,
Lord Byron

I like not only to be loved, but also to be told
that I am loved.
George Eliot
(Marian Evans Cross)

An ideal wife is any woman who has an
ideal husband.
Booth Tarkington

As one whom his mother comforteth, so will
I comfort you. . .
Isaiah 66:13

'Tain't worthwhile to wear a day all out
before it comes.
Sarah Orne Jewett

He maketh the barren woman to keep house,
and to be a joyful mother of children.
Praise ye the LORD.
Psalm 113:9

A Mother's Favorite Quotes

The house is old, the trees are bare,
Moonless above bends twilight's dome;
But what on earth is half so dear,
So longed for, as the hearth of home?
Emily Bronte

Behold the handmaid of the Lord; be it unto
me according to thy word.
MARY
Luke 1:38

In spite of illness. . .one can remain alive
past the usual date of disintegration if one is
unafraid of change, insatiable in intellectual
curiosity, interested in big things,
and happy in small ways.
Edith Wharton

Mother is the name for God in the lips and
hearts of little children.
William Makepeace Thackeray

Because I was impatient, would not wait,
And thrust my willful hand across Thy threads,
And marred the pattern drawn out for my life,
O Lord, I do repent.
Sarah Williams

It is not our exalted feelings, it is our senti-
ments that build the necessary home.
Elizabeth Bowen

Beauty—be not caused—It is—
Chase it, and it ceases—
Chase it not, and it abides.
Emily Dickinson

Put on with speed your woodland dress,
And bring no book; for this one day
We'll give to idleness.
William Wordsworth
(to his sister Dorothy)

"Believe in the Lord Jesus, and you will be
saved—you and your household."
Acts 16:31 NIV

The soul can split the sky in two,
And let the face of God shine through.
Edna St. Vincent Millay

If instead of a gem, or even a
flower, we could cast the gift of a
lovely thought into the heart of a
friend, that would be giving
as the angels give.
George MacDonald

To love abundantly is to live abundantly,
and to love forever is to live forever.
Anonymous

A Mother's Favorite Quotes

Beauty seen is never lost.
John Greenleaf Whittier

The best portion of a good man's life is
his little nameless, unremembered
acts of kindness and of love.
William Wordsworth

Be thou my Sun, my selfishness destroy,
Thy atmosphere of Love be all my joy;
Thy Presence be my sunshine ever bright,
My soul the little mote that lives
but in Thy light.
Gerhard Tersteegen

Happiness is not perfected
until it is shared.
J. Petit Senn

Things base and vile, holding no quantity,
Love can transpose to form and dignity.
Love looks not with the eyes,
but with the mind,
And therefore is winged Cupid
painted blind.
William Shakespeare

Beware you be not swallowed up in
books! An ounce of love is worth a pound
of knowledge.
John Wesley

Love is patient, love is kind. It does not
envy, it does not boast, it is not proud.
It is not rude, it is not self-seeking, it is
not easily angered, it keeps no record
of wrongs. Love does not delight in evil
but rejoices with the truth. . . .always hopes,
always perseveres. . . .Love never fails.
1 Corinthians 13:4–8 NIV

I take Thy hand, and fears grow still;
Behold Thy face, and doubts remove;
Who would not yield his wavering will
To perfect truth and boundless love?
Samuel Johnson

You will find, as you look back upon
your life, that the moments when you
have really lived are the moments
when you have done things
in the spirit of love.
Henry Drummond

The heart has its own memory
like the mind,
And in it are enshrined the precious
keepsakes, into which is wrought
The giver's loving thought.
Henry Wadsworth Longfellow

Freely we serve,
Because we freely love, as in our will
To love or not; in this we stand or fall.
John Milton

A Mother's Favorite Quotes

Kindness is language the dumb can speak
and the deaf can hear and understand.
Christian Nestell Bovee

Doubt thou the stars are fire;
Doubt that the sun doth move;
Doubt truth to be a liar;
But never doubt I love.
William Shakespeare

Deal with the faults of others as gently
as with your own.
Henrichs

We are shaped and fashioned
by what we love.
Johann Wolfgang von Goethe

For this is the message which you have
heard from the beginning, that we should
love one another; Little children, let us
not love with word or with tongue, but
in deed and truth.
1 John 3:11, 18 NASB

Familiar acts are beautiful
through love.
Percy Bysshe Shelley

A Mother's Favorite Quotes

Above all, keep fervent in your love for
one another, because love covers
a multitude of sins.
1 Peter 4:8 NASB

To err is human; to forgive, divine.
Alexander Pope

To live is to love—all reason is against
it, and all healthy instinct for it.
Samuel Butler

We love the Lord; of course, but we
often wonder what He finds in us.
Ed Howe

Talk not of wasted affection;
affection never was wasted.
Henry Wadsworth Longfellow

Thou that has given so much to me,
Give one thing more, a grateful heart.
Not thankful when it pleaseth me,
As if thy blessings had spare days;
But such a heart, whose pulse may be
Thy praise.
George Herbert

He prayeth best who loveth best
All things both great and small;
For the dear God who loveth us,
He made and loveth all.
Samuel Taylor Coleridge

You have not fulfilled every duty,
unless you have fulfilled that
of being pleasant.
Charles Buxton

Love gives itself; it is not bought.
Henry Wadsworth Longfellow

"Let us not speak, for the love we bear
one another—
Let us hold hands and look."
She, such a very ordinary little woman;
He such a thumping crook;
But both, for a moment, little lower
than the angels
In the teashop's ingle-nook.
Sir John Betjeman

Those who bring sunshine to the lives
of others cannot keep it from themselves.
James Matthew Barrie

The love we give away is
the only love we keep.
Elbert Hubbard

Love. . .
That cordial drop heaven in our cup
has thrown
To make the nauseous draught of life
go down.
John Wilmot, Earl of Rochester

If there is anything better than to be
loved it is loving.
Anonymous

If I can stop one heart from breaking,
I shall not live in vain;
If I can ease one life the aching,
Or cool one pain,
Or help one fainting robin
Unto his nest again,
I shall not live in vain.
Emily Dickinson

Love is the fulfilling of the law.
Romans 13:10

Love seeketh not itself to please,
Nor for itself hath any care,
But for another gives its ease,
And builds a Heaven in Hell's despair.
William Blake

An archeologist is the best husband
any woman can have: the older she gets,
the more interested he is in her.
Agatha Christie

When we do the best that we can, we never
know what miracle is wrought in our life, or
in the life of another.
Helen Keller

Greater love has no one than this, that
he lay down his life for his friends.
John 15:13 NIV

It is better to be faithful than famous.
Theodore Roosevelt

Constancy is the complement of all other
human virtues.
Giuseppe Mazzini

So long as we love, we serve. So long as
we are loved by others I would almost
say we are indispensable; and no man
is useless while he has a friend.
Robert Louis Stevenson

Friendship is one mind in two bodies.
Mencius

One may give without loving; but none
can love without giving.
Anonymous

For I am persuaded, that neither death,
nor life, nor angels, nor principalities,
nor powers, nor things present, nor
things to come, nor height, nor depth,
nor any other creature, shall be able to
separate us from the love of God, which
is in Christ Jesus our Lord.
Romans 8:38–39

Beloved, if God so loved us, we ought
also to love one another.
1 John 4:11

God appoints our graces to be nurses to
other men's weaknesses.
Henry Ward Beecher

Though we travel the world over to
find the beautiful, we must carry it
with us, or we find it not.
Ralph Waldo Emerson